Vanitas Motel

JON LOOMIS

Oberlin College Press

http://www.oberlin.edu/~ocpress

Library of Congress Cataloging-in-Publication Data

Loomis, Jon
    Vanitas Motel/Jon Loomis.
    (The FIELD Poetry Series v. 6)
    I. Title. II. Series.

LC: 97-75694
ISBN: 0-932440-81-9 (pbk.)

For Gloria Rennoll Loomis,
in memory of Dana Abbot Loomis

CONTENTS

ONE

TWO

THREE

FOUR

ONE

Playing Seven Card Stud with the Men of My Wife's Family

In Hong Kong I am *sei quai lo*, dead foreign devil, stink
of sour milk. Still they deal me in—the big American,

the easy mark. I bluff, bet erratically and win
the first two hands. I'd rather be a scoundrel

than an emperor, her uncle says. He speaks Cantonese,
thinks I don't understand. When I win again they all curse—

tieu lei, lan yong. The game goes on, the room blue
with cigarette smoke. We snack on dried salt plums

and lemon rind. She brings a Heineken for me,
pours it slowly, tilting the glass. She is careful

not to touch my arm. Then George—her cousin's
friend—slaps his cards down, grumbling.

Why do you choose him? Why not a Chinese man?
She smiles, circles the table, touches the uncle

lightly on the shoulder, then the cousin, then the friend.
A sparrow landing, flying off—bad luck, bad luck, bad luck.

In the Next Life

We're not in the landscape. We're locked
in the future tense. We miss looking out
from ourselves (the veins in our hands,

the sunset—its pink traffic of clouds).
We ride in the backseat, breathing
our long night on your neck. We slam

each door in the house before it rains.
Clear evenings, we hang our laundry
of stars—the dog constellation, the butcher,

the bride. We touch you at night, wearing
your lost gloves. We touch you at night
but you never wake up—not for the wind

butting the house with its blunt head,
not for the moon's long pull, or the sea
in its closet of dunes, dark suit we sleep in…

Past Lives

In this life no one's ever awake—not the gulls on the roofline,
not the seals at Herring Cove, sleek and brown as Gauguin's women—
not even the painters next door. We sleep, we remember nothing

(dark lattice of clouds, the moon's blind eye peering through).
It's late after all, nothing on t.v. but call-in psychics, home shopping
(why not combine the two? You will meet a tall stranger, buy her

this lovely zirconia ring). It's best to forget: one night your café
is crammed with Germans—they keep goosing your wife, calling
for Champagne and sausages; next you're a horseshoe crab. *Eat,*

something says, so you eat, the sea pressing down on your shell.
Now the wind's shoving its damp snout into everything, running off
with the last scraps of fog. I'll forget this, too: this body, the name

of my wife. What would I need with all that, feathered, fluffed
on my lilac feet? I'm ready—when something says *fly*, I'll fly.

Hypochondria

Cicadas fizz in the apple trees. My heart
stutters and drags. The new mole on my chest
says *wait, just wait*. The hemlocks say *Father*,

and pray in their jade hoods. What I dream
is a white room, scrubbed light. What I know
about love, I could write with my tongue

on your palm. Tonight, like most nights,
I wake up at three, unsure if I've taken my pills.
I think of our last kiss, and my throat burns.

I think of your touch, and a dark text blooms
on my skin. The doctors will weigh my balls
on delicate scales, press their lips to my belly

and blow. I'll tell them you're swimming around
in my blood. In the small owls and night jars,
the slow rain, the darkness closing its rusty gates.

Bathers

Philadelphia Museum of Art, 1993

We're not wanted out here—pedestrians, I mean—
past glum hotdog stands
                        (auras of boiled armpit),
past Logan Circle, the bronze titans smug and athletic

as Germans. The moment I left the Barclay Hotel
it shuddered and sank—
                      smearing an oily haze
on the pavement. Now there's no place to cross,

Alighieri in the back of each cab, gripping
the armrest, eyes blazing.
                    Ten a.m., heat drapes
and folds. I'm sticky with sweat, and still the wide

climb into smog, steps littered with drunks. Boys swim
in the moss-slick fountains,
                     streamlined and shiny
as seals. What if they slip, splitting their heads

on the blunt edge? What if they step on the brown
stars of glass, or the needles—
                   sad constellations,
horoscope no one believes. *All is decay*, Renoir wrote,

seeing Algiers for the first time. *All is decay...*
Nothing at all like Chatou
                 with its spaniel-eyed girls,
naked as angels, pinning their hair by the blue stream.

The Patience of the Muse

I'm out on the porch,
mind smooth as a plate—
night pulsing up

from the lawn
in velvet waves.
Fireflies drift

through the poplar trees,
so many bright
ascensions. I'm peeled

like an orange in one
long curl. Almost
emptied and still.

When the moon
floats above the ridge
like a bromo tablet,

when the mosquitos
find me (and just
the thought

will bring them),
ready or not, I'll go.
She's waiting upstairs

with her scourge
and her dark whisper.
Hold still, she'll say.

I've got a story to tell you.

My Bourgeois Life

More snow tonight
and yellow sky, rowhouses
tight as teeth. I've stopped

at a kiosk, bought flowers—
gladiolas wrapped
in green tissue, their crimson

throbbing like wounds.
Nothing bad has happened
yet. My father's alive, my wife

is still my wife. *I'm happy,*
I say, and no one turns.
My congress of pigeons

struts in the park. My derelicts
steam on their grates…

Visitation

Dawn. Dove light. Outside, the snow
blows left to right—marbles the lake ice,
scallops the lawn. I'm still sleep-glazed,

still half in the dream—my father again,
this time riding a clown's small motorbike,
me clutching behind him. We splash

through a fountain, roar down the sidewalk,
pedestrians skittering out of the way
(they were all like this, the grim

recurring car trips of childhood—
why my palms sweat when I drive).
Taxis moo. Pigeons erupt. A bread truck

swerves into the sea. How can I tell him
I'm frightened? Who knows
when I'll see him again? *Faster*, I say,

and he opens the throttle—the bike zips
down a manhole, tears through a wedding,
a dress shop, a horse-race, a hospital room…

Vanitas Motel

One room down my mother
dreams of knives. Tomorrow
she'll forget her book and run

back up the concrete steps.
At Riverside, gleaming
respirators breathe

old men; the moon begins
its long slow pull
above the parking lot—

from Arby's to the Olentangy.
I had a girlfriend who could only
come in motel beds—

the mirror bolted opposite,
in case you like to watch
or steal. She liked the thick

print drapes, the dressers
with their empty drawers.
Not like home.

Not like the white room
where my father lies, drugged
and deep, i.v. dripping glucose

into the crook of his arm.
I don't sleep much.
It's cold out, and the trains

run fast, exploding down
the dark tracks, going
where they have to go.

Aubade at Your Hospital Window

Tuesday's snow still with us, old pair
of underpants. Grackles hop
in their cassocks of light. This close to the solstice,

how shall we pray? Father, a long night of sleep
we wake up from (snow in the alley,
snow on the hemlock tree). Toenail of moon

like an afterthought. Amen, low in the sky.

Insomnia

Sleep waits in its velvet dress.
The nightbirds grieve. The dark lawn
stretches into dogwood trees. My wife

breathes slowly through her mouth—blue sheet
gathered at pale breasts. The telephone rests
in its hard bed. The dog dreams,

the house ticks and sighs. All day long,
all night the tired rain, but now
it stops. Small water ticks

from spatulated leaves. The planet
turns. My wife turns. Sleep lies between us
like an old love, longed for in the dark.

Sleep

Four a.m.—sky over Church Street lifting its purple gown.
All night the fingernail scratch of the neighbor's grapevine,

lobbing green hooks, scaling the fence. All night
the couple upstairs—
      her cries, the quickening thump

of the headboard (my wife with her back turned, awake—
I know by her neck's taut curve). Tomorrow I'll walk to work:

past Longfellow's statue, pigeon-shawled, letting the bronze book
slip and slip from its hand; past derelicts
        premonitory in doorways—

the apocalypse starts with a sour smell. I'm tired, so tired,
lugging this sack of meat. I want to grow old and forget

(was I a plum in a cinnabar bowl? The snow's toothed crunch
underfoot?) We mend and try on,
        mend and try on…

We wait for the trillium bloom. We wait for these bodies to rise
from their beds
    and fly out the window, and never come back.

Two

Hospital

It's enough to make the dog laugh, Grandma said,
after a long silence. I was reading a magazine. The i.v.

dripped and dripped in the crook of her arm. The boy
down the hall, she said. Lost his hands in a cornpicker.

The nurse came in, plump, blue bikinis visible
through tight white pants. His father brought the hands

in an ice chest, Grandma said, choking a little on her pill.
That's right, said the nurse—the doctors sewed them on.

Grandma laughed, leaned close, waited till the nurse was gone.
When they took the bandages off, she whispered, his hands

were backwards—sewed to the wrong arms. The woman
in the next bed coughed, then groaned. Look, Grandma said,

tracing the chrome bedrail with one slow finger. Bugs.

The Epileptic

       My Father
tossed a cigarette
into the rustling bamboo
beside my house
set the dry
stalks instantly
ablaze we wrestled
for the hose
we couldn't get the
sprinkler un-
screwed the
flames leapt near the
redbud tree he
hollered at my mother
turn the goddam
water off I
hollered turn it on she
hopped from foot
to foot and chirped
my girlfriend
ran out of the
house in just red
panties with a
bucket full of
water put the fire
out and several humid
afternoons went by before it
rained.

2
Breathe breathe
I said like some expectant
father panicked at the
crucial moment
knowing nothing
I could do would help
her eyes rolled up

like windowshades hands
hard twisted fins her
body wrestling itself she
growled for breath
red bubbles
rolled between clenched
teeth her lips turned
blue I tried to
pry her jaws
apart to let air
in but only bruised
her face four small circles
on the right one on the left
I failed to help her
failed to make it stop outside
the rain fell hard and

3
        now I know the
soul is only visible in
silhouette dark
planet circling its small
red sun.

Overnight in the Cardiac Unit

Who can sleep
this cold conspiracy of wires
suction-cupped and feeding
green line mountains to the calibrated screen
one and then another new topography
the ragged peaks and valleys
of the soul
my left palm tingling

every fifteen minutes I get up to take a leak
the tethered monitor the i.v. stand
tag along on small wheels (strange dogs
short walk) I doze once
until the big-armed nurse
who smells of Vick's and squeaks
on white shoes wakes me up
for vital signs

my body wants me to Avoid These Things
coffee scotch insomnia my wife
my father's stapled breastbone
knitting by the dark green sea
and most of all the groaner in the next bed
hollow voice behind its plastic curtain
calling from the well of sleep *Emmmilyyy*
Emmmily Diiiickinsonnn

The Peas

My mother passing the white bowl of peas.
Late November—already dark outside,
baseboard heater ticking itself awake.

My father's angry (dinner's late,
he's had three drinks). He's cursing
the dull knife, the roast's inscrutable bones.

I know everything. I'm thirteen.
My father's telling his one story
about the war, the Zeros like bees

coming fast and low, tracers stitching
toward him up the scarred steel deck.
He was gunner's mate—

his job to stand there, feed the heavy belt
of ammo, not let it tangle or jam.
Well I don't want to hear it again,

how the gunner's head disappeared
in a wet red cloud, how they shot
the downed Jap pilots in the water,

afraid of a prisoner's palmed grenade.
I can imagine, I say, wanting to change
the subject, wanting to talk about

anything else. I don't see it coming,
the back of my father's hand, the short
slap that knocks me out of my chair,

sends the whole bowl of peas
flying over my head, raining down
on the kitchen linoleum, rolling under

the washing machine. *No you can't,*

my father says, getting up from his chair,
flattening peas under brown suede shoes.

I found a tooth in my pocket,
he says, patting his chest. *That night*
I reached for a smoke, and pulled out

a tooth. He leans close, bourbon sweet
on his breath. *Not even you could imagine*
that, he whispers. *Not even you, smart guy.*

Desire

Last night the house was a subway train, the wind
a long tunnel it rattled through. Now it's St. Eulalia's day.
Every 15 seconds the foghorn hoots, the whole town's

muffled and dim. You're sick of these scrub pines,
this shale-colored bay—its rusting boats, flotilla
of old shoes. You want a view of anywhere else

(even the highway, even New Jersey's fecal smudge
of sunrise, Citgo tanks like aspirins dropped in the mud).
You're sick of no sleep, bad heart, the body dragging

on and on—doddering Aunt, incontinent dog.
Well. You're always complaining. The prefects tore
Eulalia's flesh with hooks, roasted the dangling strips.

When she died, a white dove flew from her mouth.
You don't want to know what the dove knew—not yet.
The dark throat, the snowfall blur. Beyond that, the light.

Buzzards

They came a week before my father died,
a dozen torn umbrellas hunched one morning
in the giant oak behind my parents' house,

wigged like magistrates with an inch of April snow.
My mother joked about it afterwards, and I supposed
that somewhere on the migratory path a big tree

must have fallen or been cut, and here they were,
our buzzards now, staring down the hill, tasting
the breeze. That oak was older than Tecumseh,

seasoned where it stood by lightning strikes,
centuries of sun. *Hard as iron*, Mr. Altier said,
folding my mother's check into his shirt pocket.

Burned up two good chain saws, cutting her down.

Last Days

Indigo sky. Bright paring
of moon in the trees.
You take your body for a walk

across the frozen lake,
past the boatramp,
the hunkered row

of fishing shacks—
heat wavering up
from tin chimneys.

The fish rise below you.
The lake groans,
locked in its mask of ice.

You can just see our house
in the distance—
Christmas lights blinking,

lawn mummified in snow.
How lonely it is
in this life—

even our bodies desert us.
Nosing off to their darkness.
Letting us call and call.

Trompe l'Oeil

Something in me wants to leap
the ribs' hard rails—wants to

gallop off in anapests. My father,
dead by scalpels, shuffles through

last night like Banquo, stitched
and lucent. And today, the bright

refrigeration of Hydraulic Mall,
fluorescent hum, my left leg

grown abruptly half an inch—
I am a hundred ways my father.

The doctor said he lacked
perspective, listened too much,

turned too far in. I say the clouds
are strips of masking tape, peeled

and stuck above exulting trees.

Communion

Mr. Yaeger's lips are pursed.
Most folks, he says
don't take them home.
I nod and sign the forms.
The rosewood box
is heavy for its size.

Stopped for the light
on Roosevelt, I ease out
the press-fit lid.
Dark ash, a chunk of bone—
vertebra, I think,
lifting its charred edge.

The light turns green.
Someone honks. I touch
my fingertip to the flat
of my tongue. Who'd guess
it ends like this?
The taste of salt, and smoke.

Ohio

Athens laid out like a meal on a green tablecloth—
pink confection of the bottling plant, East Side school
and the Hocking low in its banks. The wind sits

in the hemlocks, holding its tongue. Everything's
still as a photograph: buzzards strung like kites
above the Whans' house, sun a white shirt button

sewn to the sky. We're all part of the landscape
sooner or later. My father sings in his rosewood box.
The small fog sleeps in the hollows; soon it will rise.

Portrait of My Father as Van Gogh

He's just lit a cigarette, smoke crimping up
out of the frame. His lips are too thin, his nose
more like Rembrandt's—more snout

than sensitive beak. Bad subject, all fidget
and bluff—he won't wear the blue tasseled cap,
won't tie the bandage under his chin.

Fed up, he'll turn soon, open the door
fluorescing purple behind him. He'll step out
into the night fields, into the cat-smell

of cypress trees. Maybe he'll walk a little,
forgetting his wound. Maybe he'll set up his easel
and paint. Moon like an earring. The night's

green surge. The blue town asleep, unafraid…

Giverny, 1926

Art is art. Everything else
is everything else.

Ad Reinhardt

Monet at the bridge,
sour in his dark suit,
suddenly cannot abide
this careful tedium
of cameras, the idiotic

question of his hat,
the glass plates,
the flat, inverted lie
seen through the lens.

Monet at twilight,
walking arm in arm
with dear old Rodin,
stops to tell the joke:
sculpture is what trips you,

stepping back
to look at your painting.
Rodin starts to laugh, but only
the smell of earth comes out.

Monet in the rowboat
lights another caporal,
matchstick cupped
against the wind. He is
an old man, frowning

at the open lens.
He has seen enough
of lily pads, and this damned
bridge, going nowhere.

Monet in the garden,
hat pulled low, asleep
in a slatted chair.
He dreams of the house
at Argenteuil—

his footsteps
echo in the empty rooms.
The garden grows untended,
proud of its tall weeds.

Common Prayer

The rain fell green.
I read a poem about art.
Then we stood

around the grave, uncertain
where we'd sent him,
to which afterlife.

Lightning branched across
the clouds. A watershed.
Bright veins, stripped

from Orion's leg.
We hesitated there
like bridegrooms,

heads cocked
toward the liminal,
the chartreuse sky.

What else could we do?
Hold our breath.
Listen for the dark report.

THREE

My Third World

The redhaired baby's gone, handed squalling
over to the clean accountant and his wife.

Our lives are like a science test: your father's
hair is yellow gray. He drinks Old Grandad,

loads his guns. Everything's in season—
me and Charlie Hunsicker and the neighbor's

tall coon dogs, because they've chased the cats,
pissed the privet hedge to death. Downtown,

behind Jack's Steak House, me and Charlie
fight. I punch him, break his glasses

and a bone in my hand. Then we drink a beer.
Charlie's mostly Indian (Cherokee or Sioux,

he isn't sure), hair like a crow's wing, blue-
black in the sun. Mine is plain old brown.

2
The baby's gone. Your house lives at the top
of a washboard road. Gravel dust and pollen

sift in through the screens, settle yellow
over everything: sneezing cats, your mother's

chrome dinette. Her hair is tall
and Clairol blonde—was never, ever red

she tells us, lighting a Virginia Slim.
Later, with the t.v. on, your parents sweating

in the next room, I trace the deep new texture
of your skin—your belly ridged and furrowed

like a winter field. You move against my touch,
slowly glide a thumb–hard nipple down

my cheek, and somehow what I think about
is God, how he gets inside us like the thin

sweet suck of milk from your subsiding breast,
not quite killing us, not quite keeping us alive.

Midwest Confessional

Sixteen and party drunk,
you pin a chubby girl
face down in the tall grass,
strip her jeans
and panties to her knees.
She bucks and squeals—
What are you doing
she cries, cicadas cranking
their slow machine.
You don't know,
you still don't know.
How easy it is to forget,
and how hard.

That same night
you roll your father's car
in a dark field,
crawl out of the ticking wreck
just as the army
of cornstalks rattles
a half-step closer.
You don't remember
losing a shoe, staggering
three miles home—
frog song, cicada song—
you're Noah's worthless son,
keys dropped in a ditch.
Your wrist doesn't work,
you see double—your father
twinned and furious
in his underpants.
What is wrong with you
he yells, and you can't tell him,
can't stop staring
at his sagging pouch,
his old man's legs
veined and mottled

like bleu cheese.

After the hospital,
wrist in a cast,
fourteen glass chips
tweezered from your scalp,
you sit on the bed, still dressed—
waiting. All that night
and every night for months
you wait.

The past is a starling's song—
raw whistle, ball bearings
rolled on the tongue.
Goodbye says the father,
Goodbye says the unborn child,
smaller and smaller
like birds flying away.

The past is a no-account dog,
gone when you want it,
bad breath and tongue in your ear
when you don't.
Near middle age,
we pray many things.
Let them fly in a tunnel of light.
Let the old men look after
the lost children.
Let them sing
from the green hillside.
Let the night come again,
slow on its oiled joints.

The Last Castrato

The singing of Alessandro Moreschi was captured on wax cylinders in 1902 and 1904—the only extant recordings of their kind.

What oafs your parents were, Alessandro. Did they comfort you
at all on the cart ride home, swaddled at the groin like a Hindu?

And what did the doctor write, the old butcher—a boy
with a cancer, a boy attacked by a pig? Both true,

in a way. And true, your voice grew powerful enough, bright
and dry with its odd attack, swooping up from grace notes,

settling like pigeons in St. Peter's square. Nothing like
the pure belled tones of little Bepe (his tiny waist, corset-

wasped, once caught Casanova's eye), or the great Farinelli,
chinless calf, whose singing saved King Philip from despair

and whose enraptured followers would cry *evviva il coltello!*
Long live the knife. Still, you made a decent living.

When your father wrote, begging a few coins, you sent
an empty purse: payment in kind. Did you dream

in the piping bath, dazed with opium, that only you would live—
last of your sterile breed, pink testes squeezed into a bowl

like beans from a wrinkled pod? Now a little nervous, past
your prime, you sing to the black machine, its three horns

tall hibiscus blooms. You sing as the angels sing, disembodied,
sexless, young and not young—*Ave Maria, Allelujah, Un Bel Di.*

Watching *Wings of Desire* with a Bad Cold

We're riding the bus, we're eating a lunch
of eels and black bread. The angels walk

nearby. Tall and grave in grey overcoats,
they hear our thoughts: a neighbor's same

scratched record all day, all night—*I want,
I want.* Berlin is not Berlin. It's darker

than before the war, colder, low clouds
always ripe with ash. Each street butts

against a blank wall, tall as a scaffold—
time's little door flaps open, and down we go.

We're all ghosts, more grudge than memory,
thin complaints crowding a blue-tiled café

(stink of onions, stink of eels and black bread).
It's a long movie. Everybody wears a hat.

We ask the same questions over and over—
how to live? what's next?—until we're tired

of wondering, tired of ourselves. Sad in a way,
and cruel—our lives, the angels' reassuring touch.

Church Street

The maples open their burning robes.
Pale stars climb in the alley, zipper

of sky. What does the left hand know—
raised in a hill town, godlight fingering

down from the clouds? When I was ten
deer hovered in dark fields, coal trains

haunted the valley, bone throb and moan.
Now Christ sleeps in the vestibule,

out of the wind. What does he dream,
wrapped in his pink blanket? *Pigeons,*

more pigeons. Shoes full of blood.
Even the trees want revenge, ginkgos

dropping their slick sacks of vomit.
Cold nights in the next life—

the right hand rolls up the window,
crossing itself, smoking a green cigar.

In the Lutheran Nursing Home,
Aunt Flora Tells Two Stories

How Uncle Alvin tumbled from the hayloft,
broke his neck. How once a one-armed hobo,
a black man, split a half cord of stovewood

for a plate of ham, green beans and fried potatoes,
which he ate, slowly, sitting on the grass
in the shade of a doomed elm tree.

Grandma stepped out on the porch
with a glass of buttermilk, a slice
of rhubarb pie, saw the half-starved

barn cat nosing into the hobo's dinner—
he couldn't push the cat away and eat
at the same time. Without thinking

anything, she yelled "Hey, you, Blackie—"
the cat's idiotic name. "Hey you,
get away from there!" The hobo stood

awkwardly, still holding his plate,
gunnysack tucked under his stump.
He gave her a terrible look, then walked out

into the dusty road, around the bend
at Nafziger's woods and out of sight forever.
"How awful," says my wife. "The poor man."

"Three weeks later, someone burned the barn,"
Aunt Flora sighs, poking at her applesauce.
"We had good food then. Not like this stuff."

"Did the hobo burn the barn?" my nephew asks—
he's eight. "What happened to his arm?
What did he do with the plate?" But Flora's

gone again. She's back on the farm—fast
in her new dress, chasing the fat ducks
over the hill and down to the cool green pond.

Outer Cape Vanitas

Last of the Hopper-light,
last of the whale-watch boats

shouldering into MacMillan Wharf.
The last pink jostle of tourists,

thank God, zooming their camcorders
everywhere—the Pilgrim tower,

the 50s neon of the Lobster Pot.
Nobody's thinking of winter—

not on the last big day of the season,
Commercial Street jammed

with transvestites, bright flock—
flamingos ecstatically lost.

Last of the warm nights.
Last of the girls arm in arm.

Nobody's thinking of winter—
not even the gaunt men watching

from windows, lucent, consumed.
There's too much lipstick and taffeta,

too many Tinkerbells, too many
Dorothys, too many Little Bo Peeps!

November Letter to Provincetown

All day this aqueous twilight, *tonk, tonk*
of rain on the trashcans, half under the eaves.
Last night was colder, and clear—rats

in the dumpster, lunar eclipse like communion
taken in small bites. It's always like this,
smell of wet leaves in the gutter, short days

and the low slope of light—only spring
with its slim fingers makes us forget.
I've dreamed of the house in Afton—

tall hedge knitted with morning glory,
cows in their estrogen haze on the hill.
What if I let myself in, once, when you

and your husband were gone? What if I lay
on your neat bed, took off my clothes?
It must feel like winter, now, on the Cape—

the ocean's mumble and slide unattended.
I see you at work in your study, the same rain
falling. A mug of green tea on the desk.

Steam rising—my breath in the cold room.

Oysters

Gulls know how to open them—
climb above the bay's gray

gabardine, bomb the parking lot,
the long intrusion of the pier.

Not me—I gouge a half-inch chunk
from my palm, leave an oozing flap

of meat—blood everywhere,
the blunt-tipped knife, the sink,

the muddy shells—maybe this is why
the Talmud says *don't bother*.

2
Hold still, you say, and sponge
away the grit—you're careful, wrapping

my hand in gauze. We both know
everything's fatal: happiness,

time's pale tick of light across the floor.
Still, eyes half-closed, we suck

each fat slick oyster from its shell—
something like ebb-tide, held

a moment on the tongue. Something
like love. Swallowed whole, alive.

Adultery

April again, the wettest month—
60 watts of daffodils beside the cedar trees,
little agonies of resurrection. Still in bed,

I press my belly tight against your spine,
cup your breast in my palm. My wife calls
from D.C., sings "Happy Birthday"

after the beep. Soon, the white and yellow
butterflies will fibrillate around the lawn;
in secret tonight, the trees will all turn green

at once. This is better than the afterlife,
its empty rooms, white light. Here,
two slugs squeeze themselves across

the kitchen floor. Here, a woman could fall
asleep in your bed, could dream the old dream:
she's in the wrong house, can't find her clothes…

Illness

Late December, dawn spreads like a rash
above the parking lot. Venus smokes itself down,
stubs itself out. The house is a whistle only I can hear—

all day, all night, the wind blowing its one low note
(the windows shake in their sockets, the furnace
hammers and moans). Three months in Provincetown

and I can't tell you what day it is, which way is East
(nine hours of Vermeer's light, then sunset—
menstrual smear in the sea). Now the breakwater

sucks its broken teeth. Snow fills the courtyard:
it hates us, it knows when we're weak. 7:15, you're just
waking up—your husband's arm across your hip.

Me? I never sleep. A gull keeps working its rusty hinge.
The foghorn calls and calls to its tentacled mate.

Beach Point Aubade

When the wind aches in the pines,
and the million visible stars

douse their small fires
(as they will—as we pray

they will), when the wisteria
dangles its long green testicles

under the porch,
under the bruised sky—

I'm glad again for this body,
such as it is (stumbling

heartbeat, hair in the ears),
this body which loves you—

what else is it good for,
old dog, old sausage, old shoe?

FOUR

Leaving the Metro

We ride the escalator up into pigeons—
helix of dishrags banking around Dupont.
The bucket guy drums, night's bad dog

slinking in. We've argued the whole way home.
I'm angry, I stop paying attention and that
does it—*go die* you say in Chinese,

then louder, slapping the back of my head.
It's not New York; people stare—lawyers
scenting the kill. Is this how it happened—

Orpheus turning—yellow mouthful of sky
above them, smell of more snow on the way?

In the Year of the Great Flood

Azaleas bloomed, then the day-lilies—genitals cast in old gold.
Grandma Lula shot a groundhog from her kitchen window—
ninety-one with cataracts, she pegged him right between the eyes.

Three summers since my father died, and always the same dream:
he drives an ice cream truck, needs a shave. Early April, drunk
for the first time in months, I suddenly knew what the dream meant,

wrote it down on the back of the gas bill, then went spinning off
to bed. Next morning the answer was gone—my wife had paid it.
Now the hay-rolls steam in the valley, dropped like Geryon's turds.

Ripe walnuts thump on the hill all night. Wind rattles the locust pods—
dry bones, dry bones. I ask my father what it's like, the other side,
but the dream wanders off and I'm late for my class—wearing just

a green shoe. My wife moved out. She said when it rains, the house
smells like dog. I'm starting to think we're alone out here: the dead
bump at the ceiling like wasps—the river bloats in its cold bed.

Good Friday

Rt. 29, North of Madison, VA.

Ninth of April, rain smears from the sky like smoke.
A last grey rind of snow still lips the northern foot

of everything. I'm driving again to see my wife—
marriage a sad fit on both of us; we knit and ravel

at its hem. I remember traveling alone at eighteen,
half-drowsed in the wide, hot flat of south Colorado,

mountains keeping their blue distance, the radio
with its cicada whine. That year's girlfriend lived

in Alamosa, sleepy eyed and angry—she miscarried
three weeks later in a laundromat (God takes his share—

crow hop, jab in the eye). I think now that I just
let go, hands rising in the rusted Ford like luna moths,

long crash and roll in the dust and bunchgrass.
What do we learn, head and shoulders jammed

behind the dash, windshield chips in our fruit-
of-the-looms? Not *life is short*, that oldest news;

not *life is fragile*—here we are, flies in our billions.
It's cold outside. The Blue Ridge knuckles off

to my left, hazed, blind in the near dusk. The highway
turns to sleet. The cows in their fields know only this:

each moment with emphatic grace, rapturous, complete.

Easter

Twilight. The neighbor's forsythia throbs.
Pigeons court on the church ledge, rolling
their "r's." I stand still and they roost

in my armpits, lay their luminous eggs
in my hair. I lie down, and my wife
traces around me with chalk, zips me up

in a stiff rubber bag (off to the next life,
smelling of condoms). Who'll miss the body?
Feed me, it says—*take me out for a walk*—

like owning a talking dog. Well, come on
dog. The clock restarts when the poem ends,
and night pulls itself down like a black

window shade, and the hemlocks brood,
and the tulips finger up from their cold sleep.

The Day of the Comet

ends, as everything ends, with insects—
cicadas racing their sewing machines
(night settling down like an old dog

one dark shank at a time). My wife
calls from the city—*I dreamed of a beetle,*
she says. *When I opened my mouth*

it crawled out. Lightning tongues
the north horizon (small thunder, God
on His rollerskates). Lovely out here—

the valley, its pillar of smoke.
Fireflies rapturing up in the half-light.
The first slight wind in the poplar trees.

Dog Nights

Three a.m., still hot, the night a vinyl suit
I've worn to bed. The neighbor's coon dogs
bay at nothing from their cage. A luna moth

looks in at me, red-eyed cabbage leaf
stuck to the screen. I sleep an hour,
wake up—my heart flops and flops in its creel.

Dogs on Scatter Ridge start barking,
dogs in the valley, dogs downtown.
I think of you, and the phone rings

once. I take a xanax, wait on the porch
for its small grey calm. Mistrise. Two deer
levitate across the yard. Dogs in Meigs County

answer our dogs; dogs in West Virginia,
Kansas, Mexico. The moon bloats, sinks
behind the house (pink edge in the east,

dawn showing its gums). Every dog in China
barks at once. The planet skips from its orbit.
The dead rise, groaning, from their humid beds.

The Way

for Gabriel, born with Down Syndrome

Sleep-bleared, breasts aching
with milk, your mother scoops you up
from the dim crib because you've wailed

the whole damned neighborhood awake—
Mars still bright in the west, three deer
bolting from the yard like thieves.

Even your father groans in his half-sleep—
that dream again, the dog driving away
in the Subaru, new golf clubs in the trunk.

We live half in expectation, Lao Tzu said,
half in regret. Not like the deer—drifting back
to lip the rosebush, prune the hemlock's

pale green tips. Not like you, little Moment.
You're the dew-jewelled yard, the warmth
inside your mother's robe—proof that we get

what we get. Don't worry, the Tao says,
and you don't. Do the shoes fret
by the door? Does the rosebush worry?

Or the daylight, rising pale behind the hills?

Arrhythmia

Year of the moon snail. Year of the beach plum,
salt rose. A good year so far, except for this—

back in the CCU, my heart sprung, dactylling on
and on. A nurse wakes me, gives me

a sleeping pill. I tell her my dream:
St. Agatha drifts through the cancer ward—

breasts on a platter, offered like fruit. *Don't cross
your ankles*, the nurse says. *You'll pool.*

The i.v. drips. The hospital breathes.
The monitor's green line sawtooths off

to nowhere anyone wants to go. I dream of you
in Singapore—backdrop of palm trees, blue iguana

hunkered behind the couch. I dream of the house
I grew up in. The big wisteria blooms in the dark.

It smells like a funeral. It climbs the wooden stairs.

Separation

Brief insurrection of crows
in the apple trees.
Out on the highway,

coal trucks rumble and gear.
I sit in the garden,
watching the small still lives:

spider, stone-colored toad.
If you wait long enough,
everything happens—

cicadas crank their victrola,
a box turtle dreams
in the ferns.

The grapevine crooks
a green finger— *I love you*,
it says. *Come and lie down.*

Divorce

Half-moon. Squidlight. Fog hung like a bedsheet
20 yards out. It's a long walk across the breakwater—
gulls doze on the flats, hoping you'll die. Some nights

it's so beautiful here I drive to Hyannis, park at the mall—
I can't take Truro's boarded cottages, bay gleaming like tar.
I leave, I come back. It's the ocean that draws me—

some nights I want to lie down beyond the small waves,
let the tide suck at my clothes. We leave and come back,
leave and come back (black cat lolled in the courtyard—

Hart Crane, licking his paw). Still, I take my two
white pills at night, write the same two poems again
and again—only the landscapes change. This one's

snow on the beach, dune grass thin in its white scalp.
Offshore, three or four right whales wheeze in the dark.
Imagine, each breath held in deep water, held a long time.

Still how I hold you. Companion. Old ache in the lungs.

A Reading at the Art Colony

My attention fades, as it always does after a few poems
and I'm thinking instead about the lesbian couple two rows up,

how the young one touches her lover's back, fingers smoothing
the crisp white shirt. The rain recites its long memoir. The poet

reads a piece about his mother, a piece about New York.
The younger lesbian leans close and whispers, smiling,

into her lover's ear. Darren stands up. Pale, disconnected boy,
teenaged son of the maintenance man—he smiles blandly

around the room, shuffles a few rows back to sit beside his father.
The poet reads about birds. A child coughs, someone scrapes a chair

on the concrete floor. Darren mutters something sibilant,
like steam escaping (a woman glares—is it me, the source

of all the noise?). The poet jokes about palm trees—he hates them.
The rain sings of green fields, open sea. *Bullshit*, Darren says,

loudly. *This is bullshit*. People turn and stare, his father shushing.
Confused, the poet starts a piece about shirts, but Darren's had enough

of whatever it is—he shrieks and lurches up from his chair,
punches his father four, five times in the face. For a moment

no one else can move, even the father's too stunned to duck away—
then Eugene the big painter lunges, catching Darren's arms,

one of the writers grabs a leg, the father hugs the boy's waist,
two or three more try to help, the whole scrum edging slowly

toward the door (clatter of folding chairs, Darren kicking,
screaming shrill and wordless). Of course there's more—

Eugene is bitten, needs a tetanus shot; somehow the reading
stumbles on—Darren pinned outside in the wet grass, bellowing

Cunt! You're worse than a cunt! until the ambulance arrives.
Later, alone in my cottage, I think about art—how there must

be something to it after all. I think it might be me, next,
tense in my folding chair. I think of those lesbians, too—

their tenderness. I wish my wife and I had touched like that,
just once. The rain outside. The room filling with strange light.

NOTES

ONE

"Playing Seven Card Stud with the Men of My Wife's Family": "Tieu lei" and "lan yong" mean "fuck you" and "your face looks like a penis" in Cantonese.

"Hypochondria": Night jars are a class of nocturnal birds, including whip-poor-wills and nighthawks, but not owls.

"The Patience of the Muse": From a painting of the same title by Ronald Porter.

"My Bourgeois Life": The title is a play on Rimbaud's "Ma Bohème."

"Vanitas Motel": A northern renaissance sub-genre, vanitas paintings are gloomy still-lifes in which all of the elements refer to mortality and the vanity of temporal things.

TWO

"Overnight in the Cardiac Unit": I suffer from occasional bouts of atrial fibrillation.

"Desire": St. Eulalia's day is December 10th.

"Giverny, 1926": Rodin died in 1917. The joke is also from Ad Reinhardt.

THREE

"Outer Cape Vanitas": Provincetown has two annual drag parades. The second of these concludes an October cross-dressing festival called "Fantasia Fair."

FOUR

"In the Year of the Great Flood": Geryon is Dante's flying dragon.

"Arrhythmia": St. Agatha's breasts were cut off in the course of her martyrdom, then miraculously restored by St. Peter just before her beheading.

"A Reading at the Art Colony": The story is essentially true (this is my recollection of it, at least), although the actual biting victim was a fiction writer.

ACKNOWLEDGMENTS

Some poems have appeared previously:

The Antioch Review: "Playing Seven Card Stud with the Men of My Wife's Family."

Field: "Adultery," "Bathers," "The Day of the Comet," "Divorce," "Easter," "Hypochondria," "Illness," "Leaving the Metro," "The Patience of the Muse," "Vanitas Motel," "Watching *Wings of Desire* with a Bad Cold."

The Gettysburg Review: "Outer Cape Vanitas," "Trompe l'Oeil."

The Indiana Review: "Arrhythmia," "Church Street," "In the Year of the Great Flood."

The Iowa Review: "Desire."

The Nebraska Review: "Buzzards," "The Peas."

The North American Review: "Overnight in the Cardiac Unit."

The Ohio Review: "The Epileptic," "Good Friday," "My Third World."

Ploughshares: "In the Lutheran Nursing Home, Aunt Flora Tells Two Stories."

Poet Lore: "The Last Castrato" (as "L'Angelo di Roma").

Poetry: "Common Prayer," "Insomnia," "Last Days."

Poetry East: "Beach Point Aubade," "Hospital," "In the Next Life," "My Bourgeois Life," "Past Lives," "A Reading at the Art Colony."

Provincetown Arts: "November Letter to Provincetown."

Southern Poetry Review: "Communion."

Virginia Quarterly Review: "Giverny, 1926," "Ohio" (as "Ohio Easter").

My thanks to the editors of these journals (I'm especially indebted to Tom Andrews, Stuart Friebert, David Walker, Charles Wright,

David Young, and everyone associated with *Field*).   For their support and assistance, I am grateful to the Ohio Arts Council, the Henry Hoyns Foundation and the Program in Creative Writing at the University of Virginia, the Virginia Commission for the Arts, the Fine Arts Work Center in Provincetown and the Institute for Creative Writing at the University of Wisconsin. Thanks also to Ron Porter for the use of "Sofa Painting," and to Jesse Lee Kercheval, John Piller, Nancy Reisman and Ron Wallace for their invaluable help in editing this manuscript.

ABOUT THE AUTHOR

Jon Loomis grew up in Athens, Ohio. His poems have appeared in *Field, Poetry, Ploughshares, The Gettysburg Review, The Antioch Review, The Iowa Review* and other journals. He has received a Hoyns Fellowship from the University of Virginia, grants from the Ohio Arts Council and the Virginia Commission for the Arts, a Writing Fellowship from the Fine Arts Work Center in Provincetown, and the Halls Fellowship in Poetry from the University of Wisconsin-Madison. He has taught creative writing at the University of Virginia and the University of Wisconsin, and currently directs the Fine Arts Work Center's Summer Program.

COLOPHON

Text and cover designed by Steve Farkas. Composed by Professional Book Compositors using 11 point Ehrhardt for text type and 12 point Frutiger Extra Black Condensed for display type. Printed and bound by Cushing-Malloy using 60# Glatfelter offset acid-free paper.